SUCCESS
AND
TIME MANAGEMENT

By
Howard Wight

Dedication

To my children, David and Jennifer, whom I love very much, and who have paid a very high price for whatever success I may have achieved. And to Ben Feldman, who helped me believe in myself.

Acknowledgments

In addition to all the people whose ideas have formed the basis of this book, I would like to especially thank my assistants, Debra Ackerman and Rebecca Wallo, for their diligence and perseverance.

Second edition.

Library of Congress Catalog Card Number: 93-60310
ISBN 0-9633506-0-9

TABLE OF CONTENTS

INTRODUCTION

What does success mean to you? Is it just about money and acquiring more stuff? If so, I feel sorry for you, because you will probably never be truly happy or successful. I feel success is about making a difference in the lives of other people. Make a difference . . . and you will be paid well for doing so.

Be the best of whatever you are. I recently met a cab driver who told me that he loved what he was doing. He felt he was a professional. When he felt depressed, he just worked harder. He was happily married and had a couple of good kids.

To me, that cab driver is successful. If I had gotten into more detail with him, I am certain there is some sadness in his life. He focused on the positive. You have to focus on the positive.

You can't be successful without managing your time effectively. Time management is life management. This book is a collection of ideas about success and time management, which I have adopted from others, adapted to my own personality, and then acted on. These ideas work. They are time-tested techniques. These ideas have practical, everyday application. Most of the problems we face in life are not a result of insufficient technical knowledge. You can always find someone with the technical expertise. You can't always find someone with common sense . . . because common sense is uncommon.

Success is knowing what's important to you and doing it . . . focusing on first things first. When you know what's important to you, decisions are both fewer and easier to make. When you focus on the important, you don't have to make decisions about trivial pursuits. At any given point in time, you have to decide whether to do nothing, to do something unimportant, or to do something important.

Most people never decide what's important. There is not enough time to do everything, but there is enough time to do most of the important stuff. A lot of people give lip service to the concept of having a balanced life between work and family.

Effective people do the right things right. They focus on the important stuff. Others may be doing something right, but they probably should not even be doing what they are doing. This book is intended to help you become more effective . . . to focus on first things first.

Use this book as a workbook. Use a red pen to underline important concepts and to make notes in the margins. I will say the important things time and time again. Repetition is the mother of learning, skill and mastery. I hope that you will refer back to this book many times. It is meant to be a reference book. I suggest you keep a copy in your office and by your bed. Give copies to friends.

One of the great time management tools is learning from the experience of others. You do not have enough time to learn only from your own experience. I hope that through this book you will learn from the experience of others.

Focus on first things first. Recognize that every problem is an opportunity. Life is hard by the yard . . . but a cinch by the inch. Make it a great life!

Howard Wight
May, 1992

ABC's OF SUCCESS

- ❏ **A**TTITUDE IS EVERYTHING.

- ❏ **B**ELIEVE IN YOURSELF.

- ❏ **C**OMMIT TO RESULTS.

- ❏ **D**ON'T ARGUE. BE POLITE. SMILE.

- ❏ **E**NTHUSIASM IS THE FUEL OF SUCCESS.

- ❏ **F**OCUS ON FIRST THINGS FIRST.

- ❏ **G**OALS WITHOUT DEADLINES ARE WISHES, NOT COMMITMENTS.

- ❏ **H**UMOR HELPS. HE WHO LAUGHS . . . LASTS.

- ❏ **I**F IT IS TO BE . . . IT IS UP TO ME.

- ❏ **J**UST DO IT.

- ❏ **K**NOW WHAT YOU KNOW. KNOW WHAT YOU DON'T KNOW. KNOW WHEN TO SAY NO.

- ❏ **L**EARN BY LISTENING AND ASKING QUESTIONS.

- ❏ **M**AKE THINGS HAPPEN.

**SUCCESS IS
KNOWING WHAT
IS IMPORTANT TO
YOU AND DOING IT.**

**FOCUS ON
FIRST THINGS
FIRST!**

❏ NOW IS THE BEST TIME TO DO IT.

❏ OPTIMISM OVERCOMES OBSTACLES AND OPENS UP OPPORTUNITIES.

❏ PROBLEMS ARE OPPORTUNITIES.

❏ QUESTIONS FACILITATE COMMUNICATION.

❏ RESULTS REQUIRE PERSISTENCE.

❏ SUCCESS IS ABOUT MAKING A DIFFERENCE . . . NOT JUST ABOUT MAKING MONEY.

❏ TRUST IS THE FOUNDATION OF RELATIONSHIPS.

❏ URGENCY SEPARATES THE BEST FROM THE REST.

❏ VISION IS KEY TO LEADERSHIP.

❏ WHAT IS THE BEST USE OF MY TIME NOW?

❏ X FACTOR. EXPECT THE UNEXPECTED.

❏ YOU HAVE TO GO ON.

❏ ZEST FOR LIFE IS ESSENTIAL.

SUCCESS

That man is a success who has laughed often and
loved much;
who has filled his niche and loved his task;
who leaves the world better than he found it;
who looked for the best in others and gave the best
he had.

Robert Louis Stevenson

❏ SUCCESS

❏ **SUCCESS**. The dictionary defines success as the favorable or prosperous termination of attempts or endeavors. Too often, people feel that they are not successful unless they have accumulated a lot of money and material things. And, having done that, many do not feel any happier about themselves and their lives. As someone said, success is a journey, not a destination. If you don't enjoy the trip, it isn't going to change when you get there. Happiness lies in both the doing and the accomplishment.

Success is about making a difference . . . not just about making money. It's about what you give . . . not what you get. Success defined in terms of helping and serving others gives one a sense of purpose in life . . . a mission.

Those who tie success strictly to money are never satisfied. They always want more, thinking that more will ultimately satisfy them. Everyone can or does contribute to society. Waiters contribute. Cab drivers contribute. If you do what you do well, you can make a positive difference in the lives of others. Be the best of whatever you are. That's success.

**WHAT DOES SUCCESS
MEAN TO YOU?**

**SUCCESS IS ABOUT
MAKING A DIFFERENCE . . .
NOT JUST ABOUT
MAKING MONEY.**

TEN STEPS TO SUCCESS

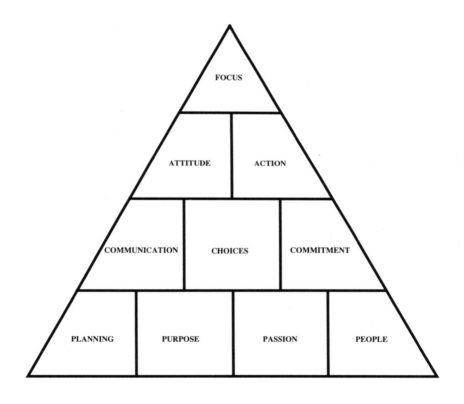

**EFFECTIVE TIME MANAGEMENT
IS ESSENTIAL TO SUCCESS.**

SUCCESS

TO BE SUCCESSFUL, YOU DON'T HAVE TO DO ANYTHING YOU HAVEN'T ALREADY DONE. YOU JUST HAVE TO DO THE GOOD STUFF MORE OFTEN.

LIFE IS AN ONGOING TEST WHERE YOU CONSTANTLY GRADE YOURSELF.

❏ TEN STEPS TO SUCCESS

❏ **PLANNING.** Decide what is important to you, personally and professionally, during your lifetime, over the next five years, this year, this month, this week, and today. Put your goals in writing. Establish priorities and deadlines.

❏ **PURPOSE.** Decide what your purpose or mission is in your life. Hopefully, it is to make a positive difference in the lives of others . . . to leave the world a bit better than you found it. Of a more immediate nature, decide what the purpose is of each task you do, each phone call you make, each meeting you attend.

❏ **PASSION.** Pursue your purpose with passion. If you can't get excited about a goal, you probably don't really care whether you accomplish it. Enthusiasm is the fuel of success.

❏ **PEOPLE.** No one becomes successful purely on his own. Success is built on relationships. Relationships are built on trust. How do you get people to trust you? Be trustworthy.

"At the end of your life, you will never regret not having passed one more test, not winning one more verdict, or not closing one more deal. You will regret time not spent with a husband, a friend, a child, or a parent."

Barbara Bush
Wellesley Commencement Address
June 1, 1990

❏ **COMMUNICATION.** The primary purpose of communication is to effect change . . . not to impress people. Combine logic with emotion . . . the verbal plus the visual. Most of the major decisions people make (spouse, house, car, career) are made based on emotion, not facts and figures. Trust is essential to good communication. If people don't trust you, you can't communicate with them.

❏ **CHOICES.** Your life is ultimately a reflection of the choices (decisions) that you make one by one, minute by minute, day by day. Choices repeated become habits. Good habits separate the best from the rest. Successful people consistently do what others can do but don't. Change your choices and you will change your life. What you think and do is up to you.

❏ **COMMITMENT.** The difference between success and mediocrity is commitment. Commit to results . . . to getting the job done. Persist. Failing is not failure unless you fail to try again.

**WHY NOT
DECLARE YOURSELF
A SUCCESS
SO THAT
YOU CAN GET ON WITH
THE REST OF YOUR LIFE?**

❑ **ATTITUDE.** Attitude is everything. Every problem is an opportunity. You have already done what it takes to be successful. You just have to do it more often. You know you can do it because you have done it before. You get what you believe you deserve. Sell yourself that you deserve to succeed.

❑ **ACTION.** Get started. Life is hard by the yard, but a cinch by the inch. Doing something does something. Just do it. If you fail or make a mistake, learn from it. The longest journey starts with the first step. The hardest step is the first step.

❑ **FOCUS.** Most people aren't truly focused on what they are doing. Their minds are elsewhere. Have you ever read a page in a book and when you got to the bottom of the page, you could not tell someone two words that you had just read. You weren't focused on what you were doing. Focus is the key to effectiveness . . . to doing the right things right. Do what's important. Do it right. Focus on first things first.

**IF YOU KNEW YOU
COULD NOT FAIL . . . WHAT
WOULD YOU DO?**

**IF YOU KNEW YOU HAD ONLY
SIX MONTHS TO LIVE . . . WHAT
CHANGES WOULD YOU MAKE
IN YOUR LIFE?**

❏ PLANNING

❏ WHAT IS IMPORTANT TO YOU?

Check Those Areas Which Are Important To You and
Then Rank Them in Order of Priority

❏ __ FAMILY

❏ __ CAREER

❏ __ FRIENDS

❏ __ WEALTH

❏ __ FAME

❏ __ FREEDOM

❏ __ YOUR OWN
BUSINESS

❏ __ SUCCESS

❏ __ HEALTH

❏ __ TRAVEL

❏ __ ADVENTURE

❏ __ RETIREMENT

❏ __ EXPERTISE

❏ __ SECURITY

❏ __ PEACE OF MIND

❏ __ POWER

❏ __ RESPECT

❏ __ FREE TIME

❏ __ INTEGRITY

❏ __ REPUTATION

❏ __ HAPPINESS

❏ __ HELPING OTHERS

❏ __ MAKING A
DIFFERENCE

❏ __ EDUCATION

❏ __ SPIRITUAL
FULFILLMENT

❏ __ EXCELLENCE

❏ __ QUALITY

❏ __ PROVIDING
VALUE

❏ __ _____

❏ __ _____

❏ __ _____

❏ __ _____

DECISIONS ARE EASY WHEN YOU KNOW WHAT'S IMPORTANT TO YOU.

THE PLANNING PROCESS

PHASE I	PHASE II	PHASE III	PHASE IV	PHASE V	PHASE VI	PHASE VII	PHASE VIII
SITUATION	GOALS	PROBLEMS & OPPORTU-NITIES	OPTIONS	SOLUTION	ACTION	RESULTS	REVIEW

❏ **PLANNING.** Planning is the cornerstone of success and time management. Planning is where you decide what is important to you, what you are going to do, when you are going to do it, where you are going to do it, who is going to help do it, and how you are going to do it. Failing to plan often means having to do something over again. If you don't have time to plan, how will you have time to do it over? Planning is the best investment of your time that you can make.

❏ **GOALS.** If you don't know where you are going, you will probably end up somewhere else. Write down what you want to accomplish in your lifetime, over the next five years, this year, this month, this week, and today. Studies have proven that putting your goals in writing greatly enhances the probability of your accomplishing them. Make sure your goals are consistent with what's important to you. Make sure your goals are yours, not someone else's.

❏ **DEADLINES.** A goal without a deadline is a wish, not a commitment. One of these days generally means none of these days. Establish realistic deadlines. If you can't meet the deadline, change it or re-evaluate your priorities.

A GOAL WITHOUT
A DEADLINE
IS A WISH . . .
NOT A COMMITMENT.

PLAN
PRIORITIES
LIST
ACTION
NOW

❏ **PRIORITIES.** Assign each goal a priority:

A	Must do	Urgent and important
A'	Long-term impact	Important, not urgent
B	Should do	Urgent, but not important
C	Can wait	Not urgent and not important

When others set the priorities, it is imperative that you and the other individuals are in agreement as to the importance of various projects and goals. Failure to understand this can be the source of great stress and unhappiness.

❏ **FAMILY.** Most people have a tendency to focus on their business lives when establishing goals and priorities and deadlines. Your personal life is part of the total picture, and needs to be incorporated into the planning process. When people are dying, few say they wished they had spent more time working. Most regret that they did not spend more time with their families. If you do not make it a goal, you probably won't do it.

❏ **THINGS TO DO.** Make a list of 10-20 things to do every day and assign priorities (A1, A2, B1, B2, etc.). Start with priority A1 and focus on it until you finish. Then move on to A2. Get started. Doing something does something.

PRIME TIME MANAGEMENT

SUCCESS AND EFFECTIVE TIME MANAGEMENT ARE INSEPARABLE.

FOCUS ON FIRST THINGS FIRST.

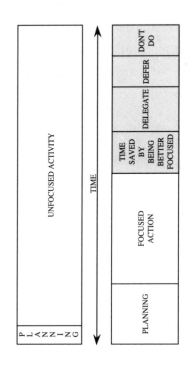

If You Can Save One Hour Per Day, Five Days Per Week, Fifty Weeks Per Year, You Will Have Saved 250 Hours. That's Over Six Weeks (Based On 40 Hours In A Working Week), Which Can Be Used To Do Other Things.

❏ **TIME MANAGEMENT SYSTEMS.** I have used the Day-Timer (junior pocket size) time management system for more than 20 years. I take it with me virtually everywhere. Most other systems are too cumbersome to take with you. The pocket Day-Timer has a booklet for each month, and each day has two pages which cover:

    ❏ Appointments

    ❏ Things to do

    ❏ Expenses

    ❏ Diary and work record

The Day-Timer also has a long-range calendar, telephone directory and project management control, all of which fit in a small leather wallet. Day-Timer can be contacted by calling (215) 395-5884. My staff uses a system from Franklin International Institute (800-447-1492) which is outstanding, but less portable. I also use a Sharp Wizard (Model OZ-9600) Electronic Organizer.

**PLANNING
HELPS YOU DO
THE RIGHT THINGS RIGHT
. . . RIGHT NOW.**

❏ **FOLLOW-UP.** When I have to contact someone or do a specific task on a specific date in the future, I write it down in my time management system. If there is a piece of paper that I need to take action on in the future, I put it in a tickler file which has dividers for each month and for each day of the month.

❏ **WHAT IS THE BEST USE OF MY TIME NOW?** Ask yourself this question many times during the course of the day. Focus on first things first.

❏ **DELEGATION.** Success is doing what you do best . . . and delegating the rest. This requires letting go. Some people feel that the only way to get things done right is to do it themselves. This is not only wrong, but it limits your ability to get things done.

❏ **STRESS.** Stress comes from doing the trivial stuff and not getting around to the important stuff. The key is to know what's important and what's not. Then do the important stuff in order of priority.

**SUCCESS IS A
JOURNEY . . . NOT A
DESTINATION.**

**THE JOURNEY ITSELF
IS THE REWARD.**

❏ PURPOSE

❏ **PURPOSE.** What is your life about? Do you have a mission? Many people define success and purpose in terms of making money. A few years ago, I realized that money was just not that meaningful to me. I redefined success for myself. Success is about making a difference . . . not just about making money. My purpose in life is to make a difference in the lives of others through my writing and seminars. You can make a difference in the lives of others, both in your personal and business life.

❏ **ARE YOU LAYING STONE . . . OR BUILDING A CATHEDRAL?** As he passed a construction site, a man asked two workers what they were doing. One responded, "I'm laying stone." The other replied, "I'm helping build a cathedral for people to worship God."

What are you doing in your life . . . laying stone or building a cathedral? When you have a purpose in life, it makes everything more important and more urgent and more interesting.

**PURSUE
YOUR PURPOSE
WITH PASSION.**

❑ **DAILY PURPOSE.** In addition to having a purpose in your life, it is important to have a purpose each day, for each call, for each meeting, for each task. Why are you doing what you are doing at any given point in time?

❑ **AGENDA.** An agenda is a track to run on. It will help you focus on the purpose of a meeting or presentation. Write down the points you want to make. That way you won't forget them. An agenda will also help you control the direction of a meeting if you provide copies for the other attendees.

❑ **WHAT DID YOU LEARN TODAY?** Make it your purpose to learn something every day. At the end of each day, ask yourself what you learned. If you haven't already done so, write it down in your time management diary.

❑ **EXCELLENCE.** Be the best of whatever you are. Focus on excellence. Here are the EIGHT E's of EXCELLENCE:

❑ Enthusiasm	❑ Expertise
❑ Energy	❑ Expectations
❑ Education	❑ Endurance
❑ Experience	❑ Effectiveness

PAYING THE PRICE.

ANYTHING WORTHWHILE TAKES TIME AND REQUIRES THAT YOU PAY A PRICE. GENERALLY THE PRICE YOU PAY WILL BE HIGHER IF YOU DON'T DO IT.

❏ PASSION

❏ **PASSION.** Pursue your purpose with passion. To accomplish anything meaningful in life, you have to have a burning desire to do it. Just because something sounds good as a goal does not automatically make it something you will really go for. If you find yourself not accomplishing certain goals which are realistically within your capabilities, then you might want to ask yourself if the goal means all that much to you. Perhaps it is someone else's goal for you. Make sure your goals are really yours.

❏ **WHY DO YOU WANT IT?** Write down all the reasons why you want to accomplish a specific goal. Doing this will generate enthusiasm on your part. Enthusiasm is the fuel of success.

❏ **PAYING THE PRICE.** There is no such thing as a free lunch. Anything worthwhile requires that you dedicate time and effort to its achievement. Relationships often suffer when one is striving for success in the workplace. This means others are paying a price in addition to your paying a price.

ENTHUSIASM IS
THE FUEL OF SUCCESS.

❑ **SENSE OF URGENCY.** Without a sense of urgency, we tend to procrastinate. Establish deadlines for the completion of tasks and the achievement of goals. A goal without a deadline is a wish, not a commitment.

**THERE IS NO LIMIT
TO HOW FAR YOU CAN GO
IF YOU ARE WILLING TO
GIVE OTHERS THE CREDIT.**

❑ PEOPLE

❑ **SUCCESS AND OTHERS.** People don't become successful purely on their own. Others help them. Sometimes successful people forget that. You don't achieve success without others buying you or your products.

❑ **TRUST.** Trust is the foundation of all good relationships. How can you establish trust? Be trustworthy.

❑ **CARING.** People don't care how much you know . . . until they know how much you care.

❑ **CHEMISTRY.** Accept the fact that chemistry does not always exist between two people.

❑ **TIMING.** Even though the chemistry may be right, the timing may be wrong.

❑ **MENTORS.** If you can find someone who can help you achieve your goals, by all means do so. Many people who are already successful want to help others. They feel that the only way they can truly repay those who helped them is by helping others. You can also act as your own mentor by learning from your own experience.

**WHEN THE STUDENT
IS READY . . .
THE TEACHER WILL APPEAR.**

❑ **NEGATIVE RELATIONSHIPS.** Get away from negative people. Unless they are your children, you have no responsibility for them. Help them become positive, but if they don't respond, get away from them.

❑ **REWARD RESULTS.** There is no limit to how far you can go when you are willing to give others the credit. When people do a good job, let them know that you appreciate what they have done. Here are some ways you can reward results:

❑ Money	❑ Piece of the Action
❑ Promotion	❑ Freedom to be
❑ Recognition	Your Own Boss
❑ Thanks	❑ Special Gifts
❑ Title	❑ Selective Benefits
❑ Time Off	

❑ **WIN/WIN.** Work and negotiate with others in a win/win context. Don't try to beat the other person into submission.

❑ **SUCCESS IS ABUNDANT.** There's enough to go around. Because someone else is successful doesn't mean you can't be successful too. Take pleasure in the success of others.

RELATIONSHIPS

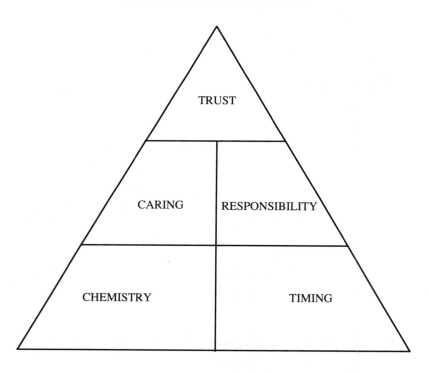

❏ HOW TO BE A BETTER PERSON

❏ WORK HARD AND SMART.

❏ BE HONEST AND TRUSTWORTHY.

❏ BE POLITE.

❏ DON'T ARGUE.

❏ FORGIVE OTHERS AND YOURSELF.

❏ USE GUILT TO GUIDE CHANGE.

❏ GET RID OF HATE AND ANGER.

❏ DON'T BURN YOUR BRIDGES.

❏ BE CARING.

❏ BE RESPONSIBLE.

❏ BE YOURSELF.

❏ HELP OTHERS.

❏ SMILE AND BE HAPPY.

**THE PRIMARY PURPOSE
OF COMMUNICATION
IS TO EFFECT CHANGE . . .
NOT JUST TO INFORM,
EDUCATE, ENTERTAIN,
OR IMPRESS.**

❏ COMMUNICATION

❏ **PURPOSE**. The primary purpose of communication is to effect change . . . not just to inform, educate, entertain, or impress. Most of the time, whether it is in a personal or business situation, we are trying to sell our ideas to others. Their buying our ideas will result in changes in their lives, sometimes big, sometimes small. It has been said that knowledge is power. Knowledge without the ability to communicate it effectively is meaningless.

❏ **LESS = MORE EFFECTIVE COMMUNICA-TION.** Combine Logic, Emotion, Simplification, and Sincerity, and you will communicate more effectively. Most people make decisions based more on emotion than logic. For example, were your decisions regarding your spouse, house, car, and company based on emotion or logic?

❏ **EMOTION**. Exhibit enthusiasm, energy, and excitement. These emotions are contagious. Smile and the world will smile with you. Regardless of the importance of the information you are communicating, you will lose people if you speak in a monotone.

**EFFECTIVE
COMMUNICATORS
ESCHEW
POLYSYLLABIC
OBFUSCATION.
KEEP IT
SIMPLE & SINCERE.**

❏ **KISS**. Effective communicators eschew polysyllabic obfuscation. They avoid big words. They keep it simple and sincere (KISS). They get to the point. They repeat what's important.

❏ **WHAT IS YOUR POINT?** Let your audience know the purpose of your communication. What are you getting at? What is the bottom line? Too often, both spoken and written communications fail to make their points because what is important is surrounded by trivia. The communicator fails to differentiate between the important and the unimportant.

❏ **POWER OF PAUSING.** If you want to get people's attention . . . . pause. If you want to make an impact . . . . pause.

❏ **CONCEPT vs. DETAILS.** If people don't buy the concept, the details are irrelevant. Give a general over-view before getting into the specifics.

**QUESTIONS ARE
MORE EFFECTIVE
THAN STATEMENTS,
AREN'T THEY?**

WHY?

**BECAUSE THEY GET
YOU INVOLVED,
DON'T THEY?**

❏ **AGENDA.** Have a track to run on so that you cover all the points that need to be covered. There is nothing wrong with using notes or a checklist.

❏ **TRUST.** When you are communicating with people, you are establishing a relationship. The most important factor in good relationships is trust. In order to develop trust, you must be trustworthy. Look people in the eye. Be trustworthy. Trust yourself. You will then be trusted.

❏ **SHOW AND TELL.** If you tell someone something, they will forget it. If you show them, they will remember. If you involve them, they will understand. One very effective way to involve people is to ask them questions, wouldn't you agree? There is almost a mental leaning forward process that goes on when you ask someone a question, isn't there?

❏ **REPETITION AND FEEDBACK.** Tell them what you are going to tell them. Tell them. Then tell them what you told them. Then ask them what you told them. Get feedback. The primary result of most communication is miscommunication, which is why feedback is so important.

YOU CAN'T COMMUNICATE
EFFECTIVELY UNLESS
PEOPLE TRUST YOU.
HOW DO YOU GAIN TRUST?
THAT'S EASY.
BE TRUSTWORTHY.

❏ **LISTEN.** Effective communicators are excellent listeners. They focus on what is being said. They take notes. They ask questions. They give feedback to ensure they understand the message which is being communicated.

❏ **VERBAL + VISUAL.** Someone once said that a picture is worth 1,000 words. Some words can be worth 1,000 pictures. You want to make an impact which facilitates understanding and remembering your message. It is often helpful to provide an agenda, a handout, or a summary, so that people will understand and remember the key concepts communicated.

❏ **SPOKEN vs. WRITTEN COMMUNICATION.** Written communication does not allow for immediate feedback. If you fail to cover a certain point in writing, people will often attack you from that angle. Spoken communication contains a sense of urgency which does not exist in written communication. If you want to get something done now, talk to the person. Confirm the details in writing.

❏ **KNOW YOUR SUBJECT.** Plato once said, "Wise men speak because they have something to say. Fools speak because they have to say something."

**OUR LIVES ARE
ULTIMATELY A REFLECTION
OF THE CHOICES
WE MAKE EACH DAY.**

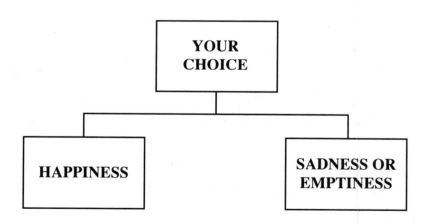

❏ CHOICES

❏ **CHOICES.** What you think and do is up to you. Your life is ultimately a reflection of the choices you make one by one, minute by minute, day by day. Choices repeated become habits. What separates the best from the rest is that successful people consistently do what others can do but don't. They form good habits and they repeat them. Many of the choices which are undermining our quest for success are made at the subconscious level. Take charge of your life by consciously changing your choices.

❏ **THE BUCK STOPS HERE.** You are responsible for your choices, which means you are responsible for your life. Victors accept that responsibility. Victims see others as being responsible for what happens to them. Do you see yourself as a victor or a victim? If it is to be . . . it is up to me.

WHEN YOU KNOW WHAT'S IMPORTANT TO YOU . . . YOUR DECISIONS ARE EASY.

❏ **DECISION MAKING.** Decisions are choices. Decisions are easy when you know what is important to you. At any given point in time, you have the following choices:

    ❏ Do nothing

    ❏ Do something unimportant

    ❏ Do something important

Decide what is important to you. Determine your options. Select one of them. Then just do it.

❏ **HABITS.** Good habits separate the best from the rest. Habits are choices repeated. Self-discipline is essential to success. Self-discipline is the consistent repetition of good habits. How do you form a new habit? Make a conscious choice to do something for thirty days in a row and it will become a habit.

❏ **MISTAKES.** We all make mistakes. Accept that fact. The worst thing about making a mistake is attempting to justify it. Learn from your mistakes and move on.

SUCCESSFUL PEOPLE CONSISTENTLY DO WHAT OTHERS CAN DO BUT DON'T.

❑ **WHAT YOU THINK AND DO IS UP TO YOU.**

You choose your thoughts and actions.

❑ Change your **thoughts** . . . and you can
❑ Change your **beliefs** . . . which will enable you to
❑ Change your **attitude** . . . which will enable you to
❑ Change your **actions** . . . and this will
❑ Change your **results** . . . which means you will
❑ Change your **life.**

Change from thinking, "I can't," to "I can." You've done it before, you can do it again. Believe that you can do it. This belief will give you confidence. Expect to succeed. Now, just do it. Now you've done it. You've changed your life. Now do it again. Even if you fail, remember, failing isn't failure unless you fail to try again. Failing is just a learning experience. Learn from your experience. Learn from the experience of others.

**YOUR CONSISTENT THOUGHTS AND ACTIONS
BECOME YOUR REALITY.**

**CHANGE YOUR CHOICES AND YOU WILL
CHANGE YOUR LIFE.**

PERSISTENCE

"Nothing in the world can take the place of persistence. Talent will not; nothing is more common than unsuccessful men with talent. Genius will not; unrewarded genius is almost a proverb. Education will not; the world is full of educated derelicts. Persistence and determination alone are omnipotent!"

Calvin Coolidge

❏ COMMITMENT

❏ **RESULTS.** Commit to getting results. If you don't get the job done, you've wasted a lot of time. The difference between success and mediocrity is commitment.

❏ **FAILING.** Failing is not failure unless you fail to try again. In professional baseball, if an individual has a lifetime batting average of .300, he will probably go to the Hall of Fame. But a lifetime batting average of .300 means that he failed 70% of the time. In order to succeed, you have to be willing to fail.

❏ **COMPETENCE.** Commit to constant self-improvement. The best is yet to come.

❏ **NO EXCUSES.** Harry Edwards, a consultant to the San Francisco 49ers football team, pretty well summed it up when he said, "Excuses simply do not wash. They never have and they never will. I don't care what the issue is. By the time you finish with all of the excuses, you are still confronted with the problem."

**WHEN YOU STOP
GETTING BETTER . . .
YOU STOP
BEING GOOD.**

**JUST TO STAY EVEN . . .
YOU HAVE TO GET BETTER.**

❏ **VELLEITY.** Velleity is the type of word I generally try to avoid, because most people have never heard of it. I first saw the word in "Getting Things Done," a book by Edwin C. Bliss. I think it is a good word to know when the subject is success and time management. The Random House College Dictionary defines velleity as "a mere wish unaccompanied by an effort to obtain it."

There are a lot of things that we might like to do if we did not have to pay a price to achieve them. You may have a goal of making a trip to Europe, but have you started to systematically save money in order to make it possible? You may want to write a book, but have you done an outline or started writing? Give yourself a deadline. Get started. Write a page a day.

BELIEF MANAGEMENT

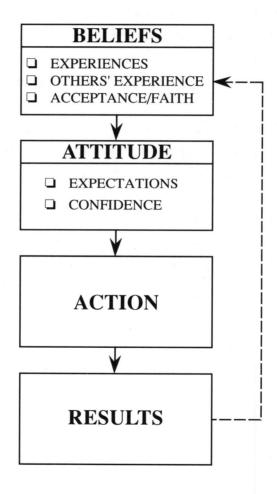

❑ ATTITUDE

❑ **ATTITUDE.** Attitude is to life as location is to real estate. Its importance cannot be overemphasized. Every problem is an opportunity. During the Vietnam War, I was with the Seabees. Their motto is, "Can Do." What a great way to look at life in general. A negative attitude is self-defeating.

❑ **BELIEFS.** Our attitudes and actions are based on what we believe. Our beliefs are based on our own experience, the experience of others, or faith. For example, Roger Bannister ran the first four-minute mile in the late 1950's. Once he had done it, others believed they could do it. And then they did it. Until the first person does something, others do not believe they can do it. Once you have done something, you then believe you can do it again.

❑ **SELF-ESTEEM.** You feel better about yourself when you do something . . . anything. If you do something, you will feel better about yourself. Doing it well makes you feel even better. Doing it to the best of your ability makes you feel even better. Doing something better than anyone else makes you feel better still. Self-esteem starts with getting up in the morning and getting started. Doing something does something.

ATTITUDE

"The longer I live, the more I realize the impact of attitude on life. Attitude, to me, is more important than facts. It is more important than the past, than education, than money, than circumstances, than failures, than successes, than what other people think or say or do. It is more important than appearance, giftedness or skill. It will make or break a company . . . a church . . . a home. The remarkable thing is we have a choice every day regarding the attitude we will embrace for that day. We cannot change our past . . . we cannot change the fact that people will act in a certain way. We cannot change the inevitable. The only thing we can do is play on the one string we have, and that is our attitude . . . I am convinced that life is 10 percent what happens to me and 90 percent how I react to it. And so it is with you . . . we are in charge of our Attitudes!"

Charles R. Swindoll

Adapted from *Strengthening Your Grip*, Chapter 13.
Copyright © 1982 by Charles R. Swindoll. Used by permission.

❑ **THE BEST IS YET TO COME.** You've done it before, you can do it again, even better. In addition to every problem being an opportunity, I believe the best is yet to come in life. It's a way of looking at each new day as potentially having a greater positive impact on your life than the prior day. Every day gets better.

❑ **ANGER.** The person who suffers most from anger is the one who holds the anger. If you are angry at someone, he or she is probably not even aware of it. As a result, the only person being harmed is you. Get rid of anger. Anger is a negative emotion which undermines your ability to succeed. Forgive others and yourself.

❑ **EXPECTATIONS.** Expect success. Expect to make sales. Expect to get what you want. If you merely hope for something, rather than expecting it, you have not sold yourself on the fact that you both deserve and have the ability to succeed.

*"The mind is its own place,
and in itself can make a
heaven of hell, a hell of heaven."*

John Milton

❏ **PEAKS AND VALLEYS.** Sometimes things don't work out the way we want them to. Sometimes I get depressed, but I know I can snap out of it. I have to. The alternative is not an alternative. Life is a roller coaster. It is a series of ups and downs or peaks and valleys. I still have ups and downs. I still experience peaks and valleys . . . but the valleys are now where the peaks used to be.

❏ **THERE BUT FOR THE GRACE OF GOD GO I.** Whenever I start feeling sorry for myself, I invariably encounter someone with real problems, and I realize how truly fortunate I am.

❏ **YOU HAVE TO GO ON.** The option is not an option. What was the worst thing that ever happened to you? Did you survive? Of course you did. Use that experience to build on when you encounter an obstacle in your life. If you can survive the worst thing that ever happened to you, you can survive most of the things that you will face in the future. Not to go on is not really a choice. You have to go on.

EVERY PROBLEM
IS AN OPPORTUNITY.

PROBLEMS
PRESENT
POSSIBILITIES.

PEROT PRINCIPLE

❏ **AFFIRMATIONS.** Affirmations are tools which you can use to help you develop a positive attitude. Here are some examples:

- ❏ I have a positive attitude.
- ❏ I view every problem as an opportunity.
- ❏ I am good at solving problems.
- ❏ I believe in myself.
- ❏ I take responsibility for my thoughts, attitude, actions, and life.
- ❏ I manage my time effectively.
- ❏ I make a positive difference in the lives of others.
- ❏ I am good at what I do.
- ❏ I am good in my relationships with others.
- ❏ I am taking care of myself spiritually and physically.

Make up affirmations for your own personal use. Repeat them to yourself in the morning when you get up and before you go to bed in the evening. Apply them in your daily actions. Picture yourself doing these things in your mind. Mentally rehearse doing them. Then do them.

YOUR CONSISTENT THOUGHTS AND ACTIONS BECOME YOUR REALITY.

OPTIMISM OVERCOMES OBSTACLES AND OPENS UP OPPORTUNITIES

❏ WHY HAVE A POSITIVE ATTITUDE?

❏ YOU EXPECT SUCCESS AND POSITIVE RESULTS.

❏ YOU ARE BETTER ABLE TO HANDLE PROBLEMS.

❏ PEOPLE WANT TO BE AROUND YOU.

❏ YOU FIND LIFE MORE INTERESTING.

❏ YOU WILL FIND PEOPLE TO BE MORE INTERESTING.

❏ YOUR HEALTH IS BETTER.

❏ YOU RECOVER FROM SETBACKS FASTER.

❏ YOU VIEW FAILURES AS LEARNING EXPERIENCES.

❏ YOU SEE LIFE AS AN ADVENTURE.

❏ YOU FEEL BETTER ABOUT YOURSELF.

❏ YOU GET MORE DONE.

WOULD YOU RATHER BE AROUND SOMEONE WHO IS PRETENDING TO BE POSITIVE OR SOMEONE WHO IS SINCERELY NEGATIVE?

❏ HOW TO HAVE A POSITIVE ATTITUDE

❏ SMILE. IT'S TOUGH TO REMAIN DOWN WHEN YOU SMILE.

❏ COUNT YOUR BLESSINGS.

❏ RECALL PAST SUCCESSES.

❏ RECALL HOW YOU OVERCAME PROBLEMS IN THE PAST.

❏ RECOGNIZE THAT EVERY PROBLEM IS AN OPPORTUNITY.

❏ SELL YOURSELF ON YOU AND THAT YOU DO MAKE A DIFFERENCE.

❏ CHOOSE TO BE POSITIVE.

❏ LISTEN TO SOME UPLIFTING MUSIC.

❏ READ SOMETHING MOTIVATIONAL.

❏ MAKE EVERY ATTEMPT TO BE THE BEST OF WHATEVER YOU ARE.

LIFE IS HARD
BY THE YARD . . .

BUT A CINCH
BY THE INCH.

❏ ACTION

❏ **ACTION.** Get started. Doing something does something. There is no substitute for action. If you take action, it will enhance your attitude. Don't be afraid of making mistakes. As I have said before, failing is not failure unless you fail to try again.

❏ **JUST DO IT!** People often spend more time rationalizing why they can't do something than if they just got started and did it.

❏ **LIFE IS HARD BY THE YARD BUT A CINCH BY THE INCH.** When faced with a goal or a major task, most people procrastinate. They fail to understand that the longest journey starts with the first step. The longest book starts with the first word. Break a big job down into little jobs, and then get started. Once you've taken the first step, the second step is easy.

❏ **THERE IS NO ONE RIGHT WAY.** Do what works for you. Fortunately, there is no one right way to do things or life would be extremely boring. Many people give up after trying something one time because it doesn't work. If the basic way they are doing it is sound, then they should keep on doing what they are doing.

CHANGE
IS INEVITABLE.

GROWTH
IS OPTIONAL.

❏ **EXPERIENCE.** Most people learn only from their own experience. The truly wise person learns from the experience of others, as well as from his or her own experience. Learning from the experience of others is a great time management tool. You don't have time to learn only from your own experience.

❏ **PERFECTIONISTS PROCRASTINATE. PRAG-MATISTS PROFIT.** Perfectionists want to have all of their ducks in a row before they take action. As a result, they typically don't take action. For example, a salesperson may want to know every possible close before making a sales presentation. Most of the best sales closes are just plain common sense.

❏ **PRACTICE.** New York cops look forward to hearing this question from tourists: "How do I get to Carnegie Hall?" The answer, of course, is "Practice. Practice. Practice." Perfectionists and procrastinators tend to practice too much. Let practice come from actually doing things. As you do things, you get better. Repetition is the mother of learning, skill, and mastery.

DOING
SOMETHING
DOES
SOMETHING!

❏ **EXPECT THE UNEXPECTED.** Always give yourself a little time cushion during the day to handle the
unanticipated things which always arise.

❏ **ENERGY.** Most people have a time of day when their
energy level is higher. When your energy level is high,
call people and see people. When your energy level
is low, do paperwork, correspondence, and proposal
preparation.

❏ **YOU'VE DONE IT BEFORE.** You've succeeded
before. You can do it again. Today will be better than
yesterday. Tomorrow will be even better. The best
is yet to come.

**"IF THERE IS ANY ONE
'SECRET' OF EFFECTIVENESS,
IT IS CONCENTRATION.**

**EFFECTIVE EXECUTIVES
DO FIRST THINGS FIRST,
AND THEY DO ONE THING
AT A TIME."**

PETER F. DRUCKER

❏ FOCUS

❏ **FOCUS.** Successful people focus. They focus on what's important. They focus on their goals. They focus on the task at hand. They focus on the positive. They focus on first things first. Much of the time, people are not really doing what they are doing. For example, have you ever read a page in a book, and if someone asked you what you had just read, you would not be able to tell them two words from the page. You weren't focused on what you were doing.

Have you ever been at a meeting or cocktail party and you were talking with someone whom you noticed was looking over your shoulder or around the room and obviously was not involved in the conversation? Have you ever done that yourself? Again, the problem is one of focus.

❏ **AWARENESS.** Awareness is the first step in dealing with a problem or an opportunity. When you become aware of the fact that you are not focusing, you can start to correct the problem.

FOCUS ON

- [ ] NOW
- [ ] THE POSITIVE
- [ ] FIRST THINGS FIRST
- [ ] WHAT YOU ARE GOOD AT
- [ ] ONE THING AT A TIME
- [ ] ONE STEP AT A TIME
- [ ] ONE DAY AT A TIME

❏ **EFFECTIVENESS**. Concentration, i.e. focus, is essential to effectiveness. Effectiveness means doing the right things right. A lot of people are doing things right, but they are doing the wrong things.

❏ **LIMITATIONS**. While limitations are primarily self-imposed, it is a recognition of reality to realize that we have limitations. To be really good at anything, you have to focus.
   ❏ Know what you know.
   ❏ Know what you don't know. (Most people don't know what they don't know.)
   ❏ Know when to say no.

"A MAN HAS GOT TO KNOW HIS LIMITATIONS."

Clint Eastwood

A TYPICAL DAY

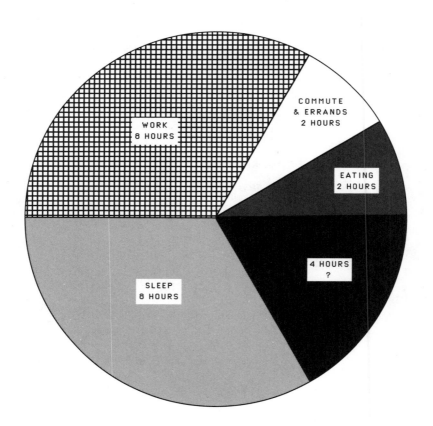

WORK
8 HOURS

COMMUTE
& ERRANDS
2 HOURS

EATING
2 HOURS

4 HOURS
?

SLEEP
8 HOURS

TIME
MANAGEMENT

TIME MANAGEMENT

	URGENT	NOT URGENT
I M P O R T A N T	**PRIORITY A** **MUST DO ASAP** • Deadlines • Crises • Moneymakers	**PRIORITY A'** **LONG-TERM IMPACT** • Planning • Long-Term Goals • Relationships • Self-Improvement
N O T I M P O R T A N T	**PRIORITY B** **SHOULD DO** • Most Stuff • Interruptions • Meetings	**PRIORITY C** **CAN WAIT** • Trivia • Busy Work • Junk Mail

❏ TOP TEN TIME TIPS

❏ **FOCUS.** Focus on first things first. Focus on one thing at a time. Know what's important to you. Do it.

❏ **PLAN.** Write down long, medium, and short-term goals. Your goals should be consistent with what's important to you. Establish priorities and deadlines. A goal without a deadline is a wish, not a commitment.

❏ **THINGS TO DO LIST.** Make a daily list of 10-20 tasks, keeping your goals in mind. Prioritize the list. A = Must do. A' = Long-term impact. B = Should do. C = Can wait. Start with priority A1, then A2, B1, etc.

❏ **ELIMINATE.** Learn to say no. Too many people are doing things which they should not be doing. Be more selective in your reading. Attend fewer meetings. Write fewer memos and letters. Watch less TV.

❏ **DELEGATE.** Do more by doing less. Let someone else do it. Learn to let go. You are not the only one who can do the job. Success is doing what you do best and delegating the rest.

THINGS TO DO

PRI		THINGS TO DO	PHONE	COMMENTS	D/L	F/U	✔
	1						
	2						
	3						
	4						
	5						
	6						
	7						
	8						
	9						
	10						
	11						
	12						
	13						
	14						
	15						
	16						
	17						
	18						
	19						
	20						

Priorities: A= Must Do; A' = Long-Term Impact; B = Should Do; C = Can Wait; O = Delegate; D/L = Deadline; F/U = Follow-Up

Daily Wrap-Up: Clean Desk ☐   Grade Today ___   Plan Tomorrow ☐

WHAT IS THE BEST USE OF MY TIME NOW?

❑ **SIMPLIFY.** Keep it simple and sincere (KISS). Don't reinvent the wheel. Standardize letters and proposals. Don't try to impress people with complexity.

❑ **PAPERWORK.** When in doubt, throw it out. The first time you handle a piece of paper, either take action then, or decide when you will. Put a dot or a checkmark in the corner of the paper each time you handle it. When you defer action, put it in a tickler file which has dividers for each month and for each day of the month. The second time you handle it, do it. Minimize the number of files that you have. A few fat files are better than many thin ones.

❑ **DAILY WRAP-UP.** Do three things at the end of each day:
   ❑ Clean off your desk except for the most important task for tomorrow.
   ❑ Evaluate today. Give yourself a grade on a scale of 1-10.
   ❑ Plan tomorrow. List 10-20 tasks and prioritize them.

❑ **WHAT IS THE BEST USE OF MY TIME NOW?** Ask yourself this question frequently during each day.

❑ **JUST DO IT**. When all is said and done, nothing beats taking action. Doing something does something.

FOCUS ON FIRST THINGS FIRST!

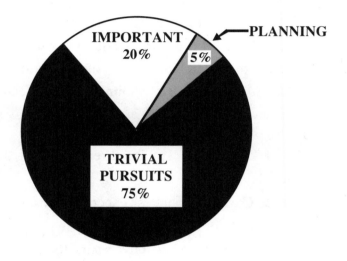

**WHEN YOU KNOW WHAT'S IMPORTANT TO YOU . . .
YOUR DECISIONS ARE EASY.**

❏ FINDING TIME

❏ Get up earlier. Use the time to plan, to think , to write, or to do a high priority task.

❏ Invest 15-75 minutes planning each day. 15 minutes represents 1% of your time. 24 hours x 60 minutes = 1440 minutes (1% =14.4 minutes). 75 minutes represents 5%. Planning is one of the best invesments you can make.

❏ Just say no. Learn to say no to the trivial things which are not important in your life.

❏ Skip lunch.

❏ Develop an agenda for meetings. Stick to it.

❏ Avoid bull sessions.

❏ Close your door to minimize interruptions.

❏ Take incoming phone calls during specific hours; otherwise call them back.

THE TOP TOOL FOR TIME MANAGEMENT IS THE QUESTION . . .

WHAT IS THE BEST USE OF MY TIME NOW?

DO IT NOW!

❑ Limit your time on the phone. Minimize chitchat.

❑ Group your outgoing calls.

❑ Focus on what you're doing.

❑ Watch less TV or no TV. Would you miss anything?

❑ Standardize proposals, forms, letters, and memos. Don't re-invent the wheel.

❑ Delegate as much as possible.

❑ Need reading. If you don't need it, don't read it.

EIGHT D's OF TIME MANAGEMENT

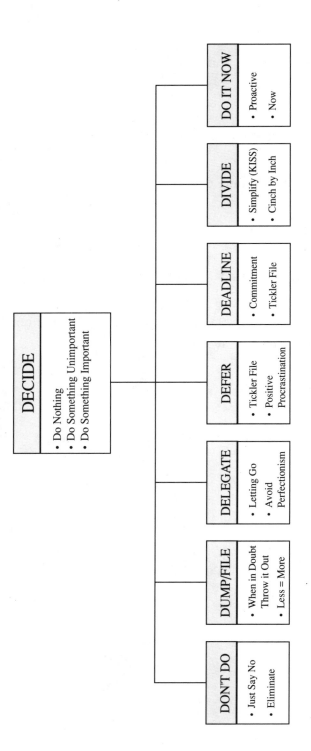

DECIDE
- Do Nothing
- Do Something Unimportant
- Do Something Important

DON'T DO
- Just Say No
- Eliminate

DUMP/FILE
- When in Doubt Throw it Out
- Less = More

DELEGATE
- Letting Go
- Avoid Perfectionism

DEFER
- Tickler File
- Positive Procrastination

DEADLINE
- Commitment
- Tickler File

DIVIDE
- Simplify (KISS)
- Cinch by Inch

DO IT NOW
- Proactive
- Now

FOCUS ON FIRST THINGS FIRST

- WHAT'S IMPORTANT TO ME IN MY LIFE?
- WHAT'S IMPORTANT NOW (WIN)?
- WHAT IS THE BEST USE OF MY TIME NOW?

❏ EIGHT D's OF TIME MANAGEMENT

❏ **THE EIGHT D's OF TIME MANAGEMENT.** The essence of time management can be boiled down to the eight D's:

❏ Decide	❏ Defer
❏ Don't Do	❏ Deadline
❏ Dump/File	❏ Divide
❏ Delegate	❏ Do It Now

This is intended to provide you with a mental checklist which will facilitate the effective completion of projects and tasks.

❏ **DECIDE.** At any given point in time, you have three basic choices or decisions:

    ❏ Do Nothing
    ❏ Do Something Unimportant
    ❏ Do Something Important

Decide what is important to you. This makes each decision relatively easy. Ask yourself, "What is the best use of my time now?" Do it now. Most people opt for trivial pursuits.

PAPERWORK MANAGEMENT

Do you ever feel overwhelmed by the volume of paperwork that crosses your desk? To facilitate the management of the paperwork, you should sort the papers into one of the following piles and then take action accordingly.

- ❏ Do Now
- ❏ Do Later *
- ❏ Delegate
- ❏ Pay
- ❏ Read
- ❏ File
- ❏ Dump

* Things to do later should be put in a tickler file which has dividers for each month and each day of the month.

EIGHT D'S OF TIME MANAGEMENT (continued)

❏ **DON'T DO.** Learn to just say no. There are many things which you should not be doing because they are not important to you. You could generate time for more important things just by watching less television.

❏ **DUMP/FILE.** Many pieces of paper require no specific action and should either be thrown away or filed. When in doubt, throw it out. Minimize the number of files. It's better to have a few fat files rather than many thin ones.

❏ **DELEGATE.** Effective individuals do what they do best and delegate the rest. You have to be willing to let go of the idea that the only way to get a job done right is to do it yourself. You may do something better and faster than someone else, but it still may not be the most effective use of your time.

❏ **DEFER.** This is positive procrastination. Many things can be delayed until a future date without having a negative impact. Put the item in an accordion tickler file which has sections for each month and day.

❏ **DEADLINE.** A goal without a deadline is a wish, not a commitment. Put a deadline on each goal and task. A deadline helps provide a sense of urgency.

NEVER CONFUSE
EFFORT WITH RESULTS.

<u>RESULTS</u>

REWARD

EFFECTIVENESS

SIMPLIFY

URGENCY

LEARN

TARGET

START NOW!

SUCCESS MEANS DOING
WHAT YOU DO BEST . . .
AND DELEGATING
THE REST.

EIGHT D'S OF TIME MANAGEMENT (continued)

❏ **DIVIDE.** Simplify. Life is hard by the yard, but a cinch by the inch. Divide large projects and tasks into smaller, doable units. Get started. Doing something does something.

❏ **DO IT NOW.** Make things happen. Be pro-active. Develop a list of Things to Do for each day and prioritize the list. Then start with the most important task.

PERFECTIONISTS PROCRASTINATE.

PRAGMATISTS PROFIT.

❏ HOW TO PREVENT PROCRASTINATION

❏ Planned procrastination is okay. Some tasks are extremely low priority or need never be done.

❏ Don't take on more than you can handle. Learn to say no.

❏ Assign a priority and deadline to each task.

❏ Don't be a perfectionist. Perfectionists procrastinate. Pragmatists profit. Most things don't have to be done perfectly.

❏ A project may be intimidating when viewed in its entirety. Slice it into smaller pieces (The Salami Technique). Get started. You only have to psyche yourself up to do one thing, not twenty. Once you get started, the next step/task is easy.

❏ Delegate. Learn to let go. Success is doing what you do best and delegating the rest.

❏ Get help. You're not alone.

❏ Give yourself a reward for getting it done.

WIN

WHAT'S

IMPORTANT

NOW?

DO IT!

❏ Write down reasons for doing it.

❏ Discuss your tendency to procrastinate with someone who you think has licked the problem.

❏ Get started now! Doing something does something.

❏ Don't fear failure. If you can do it, do it. If you can't, get help. Start now.

❏ Do the worst first!

❏ Set aside a special time for tasks on which you have been procrastinating.

❏ Take one task and start now.

❏ If you are ultimately going to do something . . . do it now!

❏ Write down the advantages of doing it and the disadvantages of not doing it.

LIFE IS HARD BY THE YARD . . .
BUT A CINCH BY THE INCH.

HOW MUCH IS YOUR TIME WORTH?

Annual Income	Value Per Hour
$20,000	$10
$50,000	$25
$100,000	$50
$200,000	$100
$500,000	$250
$1,000,000	$500

Based on:
40 Hours Per Week

50 Weeks Per Year

2000 Hours Per Year

❏ USING A KITCHEN TIMER

❏ **USING A KITCHEN TIMER.** One of the most effective time management tools I have ever used is a kitchen timer. The one I specifically use is an electronic timer that has three separate settings, and is made by the West Bend Company of West Bend, Wisconsin.

❏ **FOCUS.** Setting the timer for a specific period of time to work on a special project will enable you to concentrate better without worrying about other appointments. This can also help you get started on something on which you were procrastinating.

❏ **APPOINTMENTS.** Set the timer to remind you of your next appointment, so that you can focus on what you are doing rather than looking at your watch.

❏ **PHONE CALLS.** Set the timer for five minutes to remind you to keep your calls short. Otherwise, you may be wasting a lot of time with idle chitchat.

❏ **CALL BACKS.** When you are told that someone will be available in thirty minutes, set the timer to remind you to call him or her. In the interim, you can focus.

❏ **MEETINGS.** If a meeting is scheduled to last an hour, set the timer. If you or someone else is scheduled to speak for fifteen minutes, set the timer.

FOCUS

FIRST THINGS FIRST!

ONE STEP AT A TIME!

COMMITMENT!

URGENCY!

START NOW!

MISCELLANEOUS
INSIGHTS & IDEAS

LUCK =
OPPORTUNITY
+ PREPARATION

❑ SEVEN STEPS TO SALES SUCCESS

❑ **PREPARATION.** Sell yourself first. If you aren't sold, you can't sell. Expect, don't hope, to make the sale. Every problem is an opportunity. Trust yourself. Develop a sense of urgency. Focus. Attitude and activity are the keys to the door of success. Life is hard by the yard, but a cinch by the inch. Efficiency means doing things right. Effectiveness means doing the right things right. Don't confuse effort with results. Ask yourself, "What is the best use of my time now?" Delegate. Proper prior planning, preparation, and practice produce profits. Success is about making a difference.

❑ **PROSPECTING.** You have two prime time jobs: calling people and seeing people. Constantly upgrade. Combine referrals and cold calls. Are you asking <u>enough</u> of the <u>right</u> people to buy <u>enough</u>? Your best prospects are your existing clients.

**LIFE IS A SERIES
OF PROBLEMS AND
OPPORTUNITIES.
YOUR ATTITUDE
DETERMINES
YOUR ABILITY TO DEAL
WITH THEM.**

❏ **PROBLEMS**. Make an impact. Use power phrases and capsule comments. Ask tough, disturbing questions. Ask why. Listen. Pinpoint problems. Does your prospect care? Life is too short to work with people who don't care.

❏ **PRICE TAGS.** Put price tags on the problems. Think bigger. Recommend more. If you recommend less than someone needs, you are actually hurting the person you are trying to help. Put the price and the problem in perspective. Don't place your limits on your clients.

❏ **PROJECT THE FUTURE.** Will your customer need more of your product in the future? The problems only get bigger. The problems are permanent, not temporary. Project the future benefits of having bought.

❏ **PACKAGE OPTIONS**. Show plan ABC (Chevrolet, Buick, Cadillac). Compare. Negotiate. Combine Logic, Emotion, Simplification, and Sincerity (LESS = More). Keep It Simple and Short (KISS). It isn't a question of whether he is going to buy. It is a question of how much and what type, or which model.

**IF YOU THINK YOU CAN'T,
YOU WON'T.
IF YOU THINK YOU CAN,
YOU JUST MIGHT.**

❑ **PERSIST.** The price is not the problem. The problem is the problem. The price is the solution to the problem. You are always doing more for your client or customer than you are for yourself. He who believes . . . succeeds. He who doubts . . . fails. Make a commitment to results. The difference between success and mediocrity or failure is commitment. Failing is not failure unless you fail to try again.

IT ALWAYS MAKES SENSE TO SET ASIDE SOMETHING FOR A RAINY DAY.

❏ TOP TEN MONEY MANAGEMENT MAXIMS

❏ Look at the big picture before investing. Avoid piecemeal planning. Don't invest your money with people unless they have a good track record or you can afford to lose the money.

❏ Diversify. Don't put all your eggs in one basket.

❏ When you invest, have a selling plan. Anyone can buy something. The pros have a selling plan.

❏ Get professional advice . . . but remember that it's your money.

❏ Pay yourself first. Save first and then spend the rest. Try to save and invest 10% of your gross income. Set aside something systematically each month. Have an emergency cash reserve of 3-6 months' income.

❏ Understand the impact of taxes, inflation, time, and compound interest on your situation.

❏ Ensure that you have adequate medical and disability insurance.

**MONEY
BUYS
TIME.**

❑ Have adequate life insurance to ensure that your family can maintain their current standard of living.

❑ When your estate is large, use life insurance to pay the estate taxes and thus avoid the unnecessary liquidation of valuable growth and income-producing assets.

❑ Ensure that your will and trust arrangements are up to date.

*"We shall not cease from exploration
and the end of all our exploring
will be to arrive where we started
and know the place for the first time."*

T.S. Eliot

❏ WIGHT'S INSIGHTS

❏ Success is about making a difference . . . not just about making money.

❏ Consciously commit to success and excellence . . . or unconsciously accept mediocrity.

❏ A word, a thought, a new idea, a new perspective . . . can change a lifetime.

❏ Your consistent thoughts and actions become your reality.

❏ What you think and do is up to you. Choices repeated become habits. We are products of our habits.

❏ Beliefs, attitudes, and actions are choices. Change your choices and you will change your life.

❏ Optimism is optional. Every problem is an opportunity. Expect success.

❏ Decisions are easy when you know what's important to you. What is important?

COMMITMENT IS THE DIFFERENCE BETWEEN SUCCESS AND FAILURE OR MEDIOCRITY.

❑ What's important now? Ask, "What is the best use of my time now?" Do it now.

❑ Planning produces profits. Establish goals, priorities, and deadlines.

❑ Focus is the key to effectiveness. Do the right things right. Focus on first things first.

❑ Know your limitations. Know what you know. Know what you don't know. Know when to say no.

❑ Life is hard by the yard but a cinch by the inch. Doing something does something.

❑ Do what you do best and delegate the rest. Do more by doing less. Reward results.

❑ He who believes . . . succeeds. He who doubts . . . fails. Sell yourself first.

DO WHAT YOU LOVE.
LOVE WHAT YOU DO.

❏ The price is not the problem. Paying the price is the solution to the problem.

❏ Lighten up. He who laughs . . . lasts. Will it really matter in 10 years (or 10 days)?

❏ The primary purpose of communication is to effect change. Keep it simple & sincere.

❏ Caring, chemistry, trust, and timing are essential to good relationships.

❏ Successful people consistently do what others can do but don't.

❏ You have already done what it takes to be successful. Just do it more often.

❏ Persist. Failing is not failure unless you fail to try again. Learn from experience.

"People are always blaming their circumstances for what they are. I don't believe in circumstances. The people who get on in this world are the people who get up and look for the circumstances they want, and, if they can't find them, make them."

George Bernard Shaw

ABOUT THE AUTHOR

Born in Baltimore, Maryland, Howard Wight graduated from the U.S. Naval Academy in 1961. Following service in the Navy Supply Corps, which included a tour of duty with the Seabees in Vietnam, he joined Connecticut General in 1969 in San Francisco.

While associated with a Palo Alto financial planning firm, Howard did seminars on stock options and financial planning for such prestigious companies as Hewlett-Packard and Intel. He was an agent with Northwestern Mutual from 1973-1990. In 1983, he started publishing the Wight Financial Concepts Newsletter, to which many of the top insurance and financial advisors in the country subscribe.

Howard Wight conducts about 50 seminars annually in the United States, Canada, and Europe on selling, motivation, success, and time management. He was a featured speaker at the 1987, 1988, and 1991 Million Dollar Round Table annual meetings. He is also the author of *Life's Lessons*, a collection of words of wisdom to live by.

Howard Wight
Wight Financial Concepts Corporation
44 Montgomery Street, Suite 2266
San Francisco, CA 94104
800-486-SELL

NOTES